THIS CATHEDRAL GRIEF

By the same author

Poetry:
Hunger Games
Life Sentences
The June Fireworks
High Wire
Dark Cupboards New Rooms

Fiction:
The Blessing

Literary and Cultural Criticism:
Dividing Lines: Poetry, Class and Ideology in the 1930s
Taking it Like a Man: Suffering, Sexuality and the War Poets
Kenneth Slessor

Narrative non-fiction:
The White: Last days in the Antarctic Expeditions of Scott and Mawson, 1911-1913

THIS CATHEDRAL GRIEF

ADRIAN CAESAR

This Cathedral Grief
Recent Work Press
Canberra, Australia

Copyright © Adrian Caesar, 2020

ISBN: 9780648936718 (paperback)

 A catalogue record for this book is available from the National Library of Australia

All rights reserved. This book is copyright. Except for private study, research, criticism or reviews as permitted under the Copyright Act, no part of this book may be reproduced, stored in a retrieval system, or transmitted in any form by any means without prior written permission. Enquiries should be addressed to the publisher.

Cover image: 'Capel Lligwy, Anglesey' by Molly Caesar © 2020
Cover design: Recent Work Press
Set by Recent Work Press

recentworkpress.com

PL

For Karen
(26-10-1952—26-6-2013)

Contents

RUINS OF FAITH

Spring Fall	2
A Parting Gift	3
A Last Day Out	4
I The Supplicants	4
II Sweet Cords with Discords mixed be	6
III There are rules …	7
The Journey Home	8
Graduation at Ely	10
Documentary	12
Liverpool Haunts	13
Lindisfarne	14
Touching Gifts	16
Long Vacation	17
The Long Wake	19
O Tannenbaum, Wie treu sind deine Blätter	20
Help and Self-Help	22
Archaeology of Belief, Anglesey: Two Variations	24
I Capel Lligwy	24
II St Dwynwen's	25
A Summons	26

CRAFTING CONSOLATION

Crafting Consolation	28
Bubbly	29
A Salutation	31
Indelible Ink	32
A Gift Returned	33
Shell Burial	34
Grave Swing	36
Flight of Fancy	38
The Prescription	40

Departure	41
The Sting	42
Desperate Medicine	43
Olivia's Angel	44
Dream Mission	45
Last Letter to K	46
Aspiration	48
Climate Change	49
Dolphins	50
A New Start	51
The Limit	52
Afterword	55

I

RUINS OF FAITH

Spring Fall

I see you stand with your back to me
at the French window as you did last March
looking at early flowers
crimson and yellow, pansy and primrose,
peeping from their crust of snow,
above them, the steel-sculpted angel
rearing from a wooden plinth:
guardian of the courtyard.
In those bleak days I knew you were
reading the cemetery metaphor
of your blighted time; your death-sentence
delivered too early before you'd finished
flourishing, much less gathered the fruits
of later life; the hope of a ripe fall.
I didn't speak then, not knowing what to say
and keen to lend what strength I could to
elongate your stay. It's only now you've gone
these words insist, should I have spoken and
what said? The silence echoes in this
recurring scene of you turning to face
breakfast, the torture food had become,
and me, who could not stop the haunting
of that cold figure, the austere seraph
you'd bought, body and wings
three curved scimitars surmounted
by a featureless ball-bearing head,
apt messenger of death in spring;
an angel built to last: terrible, hard
and comfortless.

A Parting Gift

After the failed operation which spelt your doom,
walking to meet us from the Heathrow bus,
thin and pale, swathed in coat and scarf, you said,
I didn't want you to think I was ill!

After our stay through weeks of convalescence,
returned to Australia we received a card
thanking us for being there and saying
what *fun* we'd had. I have it by me still.

It was typical of your talent for friendship,
queen of kind gestures and thoughtful presents,
your wit and playfulness proclaimed:
I don't want to be surrounded by sad faces.

Your words echo in the silence left behind.
How wrong it is you can't hear me celebrate
your last intangible gift and example: how I wish
before you died, I'd said how brave you were.

A Last Day Out
I

The Supplicants

There was something in the anchorite's life
that attracted you: after illness and sorrows
the retreat to a small cell, a window on the world,
a cat for company, and maybe too the idea
of dispensing advice to troubled souls,
seeking the spirit's balm in a wise woman's words.

So we went to Julian's shrine—walking
from the multi-storey, through used car yards
across unlovely streets on the city's edge
where down a narrow lane we found the little church
and learned it was a rebuild after bombing—
the first disappointment of the day.

We had become oddly keen on Julian's ideas.
You found the idea of God as Mother comforting;
I liked sin as *behovely*: the imagination of a deity
all nurture and no judgement; the defining principle
love not power. We knew and didn't know
it would be our last trip together.

You sat on a bench and looked at the gardens.
I watched you, thinking of our childhood,
daisy-chains and *Hubble-bubble* beneath the swing.
No revelation came to us. We went back inside.
One more look in Julian's shrine, hoping I think
to feel something, a presence, anything.

We were desperate for comfort, I suppose.
But it was as if God with Julian had departed.
I felt an aching emptiness, solid as stone.

I opened the door to our last hope.
There, prostrate, kneeling, palms to the rock
a young girl at prayer. I knew we shouldn't enter.

'There's someone there,' I said. 'We can't intrude.'
You didn't argue. We left. Somehow, I knew
the girl was praying for her dying mother.
In that attitude of despair and faith I saw all our longing.
As you drove us home, the back of a bus boasted
we'd win the war on cancer. 'I've lost,' you said.

No miracle. No escape. As for Julian's wisdom:
how we cling to the idea of a saving love,
our lips pressed to the cobbles, we crave belief.
I'm left with the sight of you on that garden bench,
ill and thin and dying beyond stone,
the anchorite's spirit alive in you, reaching for me.

II

Sweet Cords with Discords mixed be

After Julian's shrine, Norwich Cathedral,
too monumental, too cold, too impersonal
to offer anything like comfort.
It spoke in stone of voiceless generations
who worked and worshipped with little reward
and are dust. But then we came upon
the plaque to Osbert Parsley, who served
the Church as singing man and boy
for over sixty years. Of humble origin
he navigated the risky turmoil of the Reformation
wrote music for both Latin and English rites
eschewing the futility of dogma.
You loved his name. We agreed I should
be inspired to avoid the brutality of politics
in Church or State and strive to make words
rise above parliament, press or pulpit:
echoing in the vault, trust the song to sing its love.

III

There are rules . . .

In Norwich cathedral café for lunch,
you fancied a scone with jam and cream.
It seemed a choice of some extravagance
given your troubled digestion, not to mention diabetes,
but this was the point I guess: a moment
of audacious celebration in honour of our day out.

But when you asked, the woman said you could
have a scone with jam but no cream. They didn't serve
cream until tea-time at three o' clock. I wanted
to scream, *Can't you see she's dying. What can such
pettiness mean?* Instead, we made another polite request,
surely she could make an exception just this once.

No, she couldn't. Mrs Jobsworth had her way.
Compliant and defeated we endured our lunch.
I struggled with forgiveness. Nothing that day
had been as it should. Faith seemed a mystical
delusion. I missed the anchorite's graceful whisper:
don't seek for solace or compassion in stone places.

The Journey Home

For John and Lynne Mercer

From a train window, landscape unrolled
like a dream I once had of summer;
folds of emerald fields under a June sun,
Friesian cows, hedgerows.
A mystery how we by-passed
the industrial detritus I'd expected,
the decaying factories and warehouses
of Birmingham and Wolverhampton.
It was as if all had been made new—or old—
I passed through a rural England, an idyll:
I wondered if I could ever call it home.

I was travelling north for a funeral.
The night before, my dying sister wept
saying she didn't want me to go.
I knew her tears were not about
my journey but that longer leaving,
which beckons all without reprieve.
I was pledged in friendship to attend
the last farewell of another mother.
In a shabby fifties church that might
become a bingo hall, I heard
a son speak of modesty and grace.

How Elsie gave a lot and demanded little,
though widowed twice, alone for many years,
practised her talent for contentment,
enjoyed her grand-kids and her Christmas sherry,
knew how to laugh and quietly scorn
the ambitious follies of the world.
I remembered her gentle face and eyes,
the colour of pale violets in spring.
Old women formed an honour guard,

as she was shouldered by descendants
who took their true bearings well.

On the return trip I saw those fields again
bathed now in gold and shadow,
through them wound an old canal,
a barge, a man solitary at the tiller,
I cannot say how strange it seemed
as if he and I were travelling out of time
into some vast beyond where all was peace;
and later, with the light fading to dusk,
in a crease of hills with reference to nothing,
beyond reason, a gloss on *all must suffer*,
a vacant cross against the charcoal sky.

Graduation at Ely

I am exploring this cathedral grief
where you stood robed in triumph
blue and saffron to receive the degree
which meant so much: *It's my Olympic gold,*
you said, despite your diagnosis,
the shadow of impending death
now imminent, darkening on you.
And always in the shafts of stony light
I'll see you turn and smile at me
in the front row at last for once
your face a vision of delight as in
our childhood conspiracy, our club of two,
you handing out the merit badges
I didn't deserve. The organ boomed;
I hoped a better tune might wreath the march
toward the great octagonal lantern
where Christ in glory looks down on ours,
but still the notes were grand enough
to introduce the moment of your citation,
doffed caps, the doctoral scroll in hand,
the all too brief applause. Then it was done
and we sat on through the naming
of a hundred Bachelor graduands,
the exhaustion of acclaim by rote,
your happy moment dulled by repetition.
I wished it all could be for you alone
your last hurrah echoing on and on
instead of some grim parable about pride;
the vaulted ceiling and flying buttresses designed
to remind us who and what we are
our smallness in that cavernous nave;
all of us dying and destined for dust.
Now, as I write these wandering lines,
I conjure the faithful builders,

generations of master masons whose lives
became this stone Ship of the Fens;
how little my making seems against
their vast and lasting vessel. Yet it refuses
me passage back to the reality of you;
that beatific smile; our lovely friendship.
Instead, I inhabit this hollowed space,
the congregation of friends departed,
your ghostly presence hovering here and not here,
there and not there, against the blank of loss;
and yet and yet such is the place of prayer,
becoming this poor hymn and doubtful liturgy,
blocks of my hope and my despair,
which do not tower, but still aspire
to sing the possibility of spirit: your lasting shine.

Documentary

There always had to be photographs—
a parental obsession at every gathering,
Christmas, birthdays, anniversaries,
however fraught or awkward the occasion,
however clear the divisions and disasters,
posing for the corrective lens
we always were and are a happy family.
And so you stood, graduation scroll in hand,
your thin figure wreathed in the doctoral gown,
a dying smile not quite managing
to disguise however hard you tried,
the yearning in your anguished eyes,
while we did our best in portrait groups
to pretend we didn't know your demise
was imminent, or if we knew to let
the seeming unreality transcend our fear.
We all wanted to look joyful for your sake,
for our sake, yet in those final shots
the camera refused to lie or heal
and left us with our failed evasions
frozen in each memorial frame.

Liverpool Haunts

We travel the old dock road beyond the pier-head
rehearsing famous names: Gladstone, Sandon, Wellington,
dead squares of vacant water behind blank walls;
the clock on the abandoned harbour master's tower
tells no one's time stuck in a never ending past,
while rusting gantries and skeleton sheds,
the long dis-used railway lines criss-crossing the street
lead to blood-house pubs boarded with steel
corrugations; all that's left of living trade are
ghosts of its hey-day, the ships moored three deep;
the thoroughfare alive with steam wagons, sailors, dockers,
the bustle of high adventure and enterprise.
How it all becomes a broken landscape of desire
as if to say here all endeavour and ambition ends;
even the renovations don't convince;
the old warehouses re-built to luxury flats
look like places of correction in which
the wealthy owners are sentenced to a long stretch,
each night's lonely escape from the humdrum day
haunted by voices raised in capstan shanties,
dreams of rich voyages, girls in every port
and, at the end, love in safe harbour. They wake
to the modern city marooned in its future;
from their barred windows see brave concrete,
steel and glass rearing from ruin, jousting with decay.

Lindisfarne

On Holy Island tourists chirrup
like birds among the ruins;
the floors of the Abbey are grass,
flowers bloom from broken walls,
while sky pours through abbreviated arches.
The builders are still implicit here,
trowelling faith day after day,
heaving their material prayer
beyond themselves block by block
towards heaven, pledging body, soul
psyche to this remote project,
hoping to channel power and raise
from earth a stone hymn.
I stand and listen for the echo.
Twelve monks raise their voices
enclosed in ethereal vespers,
while the sound of the sea
creeps through draughty windows,
God's whisper sighing all night
the promise of cold eternity.
What longing stalked their dreams?
What erotic impulse moved their
sleeping hands, palming praise of
fragile flesh only to re-discover
each morning the haunted crucifix
with its promise of nails and grace,
that ancient recipe for suffering?
Family groups stare and wander;
next they will walk to the castle,
which stands intact upon the headland,
proud, as if to emphasise we still fight
but rarely pray; soldiers of the cross,
their anger, never far enough away.
So I find I'm thankful for the cracked

shell of this sanctuary, which seems to admit
in its lasting case, a more compelling
reason to rejoice; the emerald carpet,
wallflowers and birdsong calling us
to re-invent and praise a gentler One,
some goddess in harmony with broken stone,
who might inspire a sensuous psalm
to love not rule; Brigid, say, or Flora:
She who nurtures pleasure and makes new.

Touching Gifts

Two photos of us as children holding hands—
one the day I started school wearing my too big blazer
its golden badge: *Queen's Road Primary School.*
Two years ahead of me, still we'd walk together;
you protected me from schoolyard bullies
and taunting girls, ever after saw yourself
as my champion and protector.
The other photo, aged six and eight, we're in the sea
jumping waves on a family holiday
me shrivelled up with cold, shoulders hunched
head down and giggling, while you are head up
and smiling, square shouldered to the lens
in ballet pose. Just so, I always thought of you
as the stronger, brighter, more graceful one
despite the blows life dealt you; your lost first love,
chronic illness, then this last calamity.

I held your hand at chemo and again
when they needled you, draining fluid
from your abdomen. In extremity
like most unbelievers, I suppose,
I prayed, too late perhaps, though it seems
there's nothing much a loving God can do
with pancreatic cancer—the price of freedom
in this world, some theologians say:
love being at cross purposes with power.
And yet one supplication was granted—
at the last I was allowed to hold your hand
until your final breath, though I don't know
if you could tell or if somewhere in those
obscure last depths you joined with me again
showing the way to cross safely,
jumping breathless in the waves.

Long Vacation

As you lay dying somewhere beyond speech,
your eyes green as pale sea stones still
gazed into the distance, searching, as if
trying to understand what lay before you.
I tried hard to hope with that look of puzzled wonder
you discerned the lights of paradise
beckoning to a place where all bewilderment
might disappear: the meaning of our suffering
made plain. Instead, I fear you were trying
to fathom the hideous photo on the wall
at the end of your bed, a print like some
cheap travel agent's poster advertising
a miraculous getaway; it figured
in Dulux white a long and empty jetty,
a palm tree or two, the blank of sea and sky
two shades of witless blue. Someone's
daft idea of heaven. I imagined
what you'd say if you could see it,
you who loved holidays and insisted,
if you insisted ever, on aesthetic pleasure,
'If that's Elysium forget it, let me
go to Rome or Venice or if we're talking
beach, give me surfing at Woolacombe
or collecting shells at Barricane every time.'
I can hear your delighted irony,
your sparkle like water drops on your hair
as you rose from the sea when we were kids.
But that was gone forever as I watched
each day your restless peering and
at the end, the quiet close, the stillness.
I hope it felt like the great escape
taking the all-night sleeper to a place
where every wave is well-caught and gives
the long rush and ride to peaceful shallows,

and the smallest shells on every beach
whisper wise consolations viz God's
creativity with playful particles.
Meanwhile, I'm left with memories of
that picture on the wall and these
imperfect words, which cannot reach you
and might as well be some catchy slogan,
pleading like a desperate advert,
wishing I could give you that vacation
of a lifetime here in Australia
as we'd planned before your diagnosis,
and extract a parting promise,
come visit us again sometime soon.

The Long Wake

In the tombs of the Han Kings
there were entertainment rooms
to host the parties of the after-life;
vessels were left with food and wine,
jade ornaments, terra cotta figurines:
musicians and dancers, who, strangely
would come alive to join the magic
revels of an endless night.

In Cambridge for your birthday bash,
we saw the exhibition at the Fitz;
my favourite figure was the dancing man,
his body in robes a flowing 'S', his arms
dynamic arches with flounced sleeves;
I admired the too-expensive souvenir,
instead acquired a guide in which he graced
The Search for Immortality.

After you died, your friend the chaplain said
she often thought of heaven as a party
where all the lost would be found again—
in bliss we'd celebrate with those we loved—
this in the room, where, only months before
we'd laughed and champagne-toasted you:
more like forty than sixty we all agreed;
when life begins, I said.

He was my last Christmas present from you:
the Chinese dancing man. I have him by me
on my desk and every day I see his smile
captured still, until he comes to life once more.
Two thousand years and continents apart
the same strange sorcery weaves and teases:
I rehearse what it would be to see you again—
the party we'd have; what dancing then.

O Tannenbaum,
Wie treu sind deine Blätter

No Christmas tree this year.
Twinkling lights on shining tinsel,
the determined gaiety of gaudy baubles,
glass bells and plastic angels,
the fragile origami star,
too sad reminders of past magic
and that last festive season
your illness just announced.
You were invited to carols at King's,
a walk through the frost-stilled night;
how thrilled you were to hear the boy's
treble soar to the vaulted height,
echoing like some lost spirit's
searching cry, ethereal and unnerving.
You spoke to me of how you cried
in memory of earlier joyful times
amid the English winter gloom.
You loved it all—mince pies, mulled wine,
the glitter and ribboned bows on gifts
in honour of the birth made sacred;
how you thought yourself blessed
among women and how you strove
to make the season special for your boys.
That last Twelfth Night you phoned, distressed
because you had to pack away
the decorations; sad stripping back
to the naked tree, its yellowing green
needles falling in a dying fall.
I knew you thought it was your last time,
the same tearing down of all delight,
fragile flesh and bone and soul laid bare,
though I tried to persuade you it wasn't so
peddling hope, until all hope was gone.

I see now I was lost in denial, praying
for the saving miracle that never came.
No Christmas tree this year, but words instead:
a pledge, K, one day I will learn to liberate
my grief and generate some lasting sparkle
to keep my needling memories of you evergreen.

Help and Self-Help

for Revd. Deborah McVey

After my sister's death,
bereft in the suburban café,
you comforted me as you
comforted my sister when
she heard there was to be no miracle
cure. You led her funeral service
wearing your rainbow stole,
speaking the words of nature's
peace, an idea of sacred process.
Back in the café you took my hand
and spoke extempore from the Old Book,
casting these lovely lines:
Fear not. You are beloved
I am with you, you are mine,
I have called you by your name.
I can't say how deep those words
reached into me, so in need I was
of mythical, magical thinking,
butting against vacant mystery.
And in your eyes I saw a light
shining inside out, I knew you
were neither sentimental
nor fanatical; in that moment
you were the good God-mother to me.
I spoke of my wrestle with
the place of suffering;
how the cross might become
a spur to sado-masochism;
remembered Gascoyne's
Christ of Revolution and of Poetry;
the difficulty of reconciling
love and power to forge
a politics of compassion.

You remarked how spiritual
my sister was. I wondered
how much good it did her,
but didn't voice my bitterness
not wishing to disappoint you,
the gentlest, kindest fisher of people.
My mental strife is mine alone:
struggling towards some new becoming,
how I wriggle and squirm against the hook.

Archaeology of Belief, Anglesey: Two Variations

For Richard

I

Capel Lligwy

Always it seems the roof is first to go,
the beams leached by coastal weather.
These ancient churches offer no hiding place,
they harbour space and through their ruined arches
long perspectives of the sea and blank horizons.
The summoning bell is absent. No singing
but the wind's play upon wild grass.
The comforts of old faith, if comforts they were,
are worn to cold stone. Inside, derelict,
the forlorn cross is propped, austere and grave
as the remains of faith beckoning:
the wreckage plain upon the headland.

II

St Dwynwen's

Ruins of faith
the gaping walls of Llanddwyn
patron saint of love
a cross still visible through the broken arch
light where once a bell rang clear
across the island.

Undogmatic
this opening to sky
the sea's hymn, a possibility.
What, after all, is this?
A reaching for benediction
with words for stone . . .

Cement holds
the crumbling edifice
refusing to sink to earth,
storm-light and gale howl through the nave
swelling the choir
to a ferocious amen.

A Summons

I dreamt I was invited to God's funeral;
I hadn't been reading Nietzsche.
The death of the author had reached my ears
from hallowed halls of learning;
I'd even muttered obsequies myself
along those lines, but this was something
else entirely. I tried to imagine the service
and what circumstances would persuade
me to attend. After all, I'd not been close
for years, more a distant hopeful caller
to an obscure address in the suburbs
of Unknowing, the replies to which
had been ambiguous at best
until this visitation in dark times,
which sets me up to resist the implications;
after all, who wrote the invitation?
I imagine the music to be played:
Mozart, Bach, some Arvo Pärt, perhaps
to make it modern, and words, biblical of course,
Donne and Herbert maybe for support;
Eliot too conservative I'd like to think,
but Wystan Hugh might get a guernsey.
I wax fanciful I know, but here's the point:
surely to give me pause and show me
a whimsical theology;
a sense of humour sacred to the task
of re-creation; now I've teased
the meaning of this summons out:
each fertile God, like us, is born to die,
so we might dream of resurrection;
that's what they're *for*; their rites of passage
like our own, designed to glorify
the start of a slow movement
from lamentation to sure praise.

II

CRAFTING CONSOLATION

Crafting Consolation

For Revd. Paula Spalding

Your kind friend sent a condolence card
and in the envelope a small white feather
which, she said, seemed to come from nowhere.
Angel's wings obviously, I wrote in my reply.
And for days after, everywhere I went
I found small replicas, as if some tiny
feathered thing had scattered its moulting
on urban pavements, in shops and unlikely
bathrooms, as well as in gardens shocked
with loss. I fingered the delicate plumes
and hoped they were tokens from some
unlikely messenger, saying you were safely
wrapped in God's eiderdown—how reason is
undone by grief. Later, in answer
to my penned bewilderment a suggestion:
Death is like a going home.
I want to believe, but if that were so,
surely you'd like us to be there too
not left out here puzzling in the cold,
trying to fashion from nature's casual
droppings a scarecrow angel,
like children gluing tufts to lolly sticks,
who dream of trumpets announcing
a perpetual Christmas and forget
the frozen shepherds cowering
as they stare at the inexplicable
in the pitch black night.

Bubbly

How you loved all things that sparkle,
fairy lights, jewellery and champagne
mirror of your brilliance pitched against
the dour values of our inheritance—
a world shaped by depression
and two wars: duty, work, endurance
was the creed; pleasure rationed
and contained; unseemly behaviour
was anathema; *button up*
an answer to more than cold.
No wonder you were moody like me,
still in company you could effervesce
and light a room with radiant wit:
'My word, your sister's a lively girl,'
my friend, the poet, said in admiration
of brisk scintillations over dinner.
How quick you were with the zest
of irony; how often you delighted
to make fun of me, my plodding tongue;
no surprise another favourite was
lemon in fizzing tonic with dry gin,
the last drink I made for you
that day in the summer courtyard
when all you wanted was to be *normal*
and enjoy the sun and friends and the
geraniums you'd planted and the ceramic
lizard crawling the walls—a Mediterranean
feel you said—and we spoke of your PhD
lately acquired and papers given and
nobody mentioned the book you'd hoped to write
knowing now it would not be done
yet unaware how soon you'd up and be gone.
Outside our front door we've planted an Azalea
called *Pink Bubbles,* as if in all our goings

and returns to raise a toast in celebration
of your life's sweet fizz, though in our remembering
we view the glass abandoned at party's end
and grit our teeth to bear grief's flat astringent drops.

A Salutation

For Pauline Sutton

Some months after the funeral,
checking e-mails from the other hemisphere,
there's one from Pauline; subject: *Hell.*
It's not promising. My mind traverses
the last five years, their litany of loss—
a son, two friends and mentors,
then you, lovely sister, and like some grim
comedic postscript even Frankie
the cat succumbed. Suffice to say
I'm well acquainted with grief.
So on a bright morning of frost sparkle
and sunshine I don't want more bad news.
Through the window I watch parrots cavort,
hunger's casual gymnasts in the trees,
squawking over breakfast to celebrate
the playful day. *Coraggio* my own word
to you dying limps back to me
battered and bruised; I open the message
from your friend. It speaks of planting
wild primroses on your grave
and how the site at Barton Glebe
is bright with daisies and dandelions
peaceful as ever. There is talk
of daily things and at the last:
Tell Claire K's rose is blooming.
As I felt the familiar watering begin,
I realised the typo in the subject bar:
Hello it should have said. And saw how that
single 'o' could hold at once the meaning
of love perfected or the blank of absence,
the nothing of death we try to fill with heaven.
And in my mind against the parrot's raucous din
as if to reassure I should dwell on more than zero
I swear I heard your voice make greeting.

Indelible Ink

As if you knew you would not be writing again,
the pens you left have little ink in them.
Of all the things I would have liked
these are they. You knew of course—
no words needed—not even a jest about
my previous disregard for delicate implements;
the way as a boy I'd write with a bendy refill
having destroyed the plastic biro shell.
And so on a spring day in Sydney
from an old-fashioned shop you would have loved
I bought ink and refills—the vendor in bow tie
and braces asked if I preferred black or blue.
I hesitated knowing either would do
for bruises—to pen the unfolding grief
of losing you, and before my eyes I saw
as every day I seem to, your handwriting
on letters, cards, the fly leaf of so many books,
always in blue for the virgin's gown and
clear skies you loved; how often I thought
Australia should have been your place,
though English restraint became you;
how you hated all that drab damp weather
and longed for summer holidays,
sending gleeful postcards full of sun.
Black, I chose, so I would not remind myself
with every word of all your loving gifts
and greetings never more to be received;
my mourning colour a tribute to
the everlasting blues you've left.

A Gift Returned

For Andrew and David

I'm glad it's me not either of the boys,
you said, *I'd rather be the one to die.*
Beside your intellectual life,
motherhood was a sacred task for you
– no accident your stairwell muse—
a tapestry placed so each ascent was met
by Flora via Morris and Burne-Jones:
I am the handmaid of the earth. Just so,
domestic goddess, you scattered gifts,
maker and baker of daily feasts,
cook and cleaner and garden builder;
those last days in June how anxious you were
to pot the bright geraniums for summer
in courtyard and back patio: their bloom
outlasting you, as your boys live to mourn
your early passing, though surely something
of your abundance lives in them, in us,
husband, sons, father, brothers,
who bore the weight of your wicker casket
to the woodland burial at Barton Glebe,
no cremation for you, who wanted to grow
back to the mothering earth; to live
amid the birdsong and wild flowers,
scattering forth again as we sow your plot
and water our mourning seeds for you
to *broider fair* your lasting gown.

Shell Burial

for my grand-daughter, Charlotte

Without bucket or spade we build
the sandcastle, dragging and gathering,
piling and patting our little Camelot.
I excavate a moat, shape a drawbridge,
a sloping road leading to the keep,
while you look for shells to decorate
the edifice, or so I thought, the way we'd
done last holiday some months ago.
But this time you have another purpose:
instead of rendering the fort,
silently intent you bury your trove
beneath the road; push fans and whorls
and spirals deep inside the solid mound,
your tiny fingers busy smooth the surface
concealing wonder beneath the bland
façade. It is no aberration.
You run to collect more. Again and again,
you bury your haul deep within,
as if approaching four years old
you already know the maker's secret;
the way charged moments sink
from the world to be saved in the dark
protected as a scallop in the shell,
the shell within the sandy walls.
The next stage of delight is to uncover
to see again unearthed the treasure
and recognise the prompting gift
for what it is; to clean and polish
and make new. I watch you brush away
the grit and know you have begun
the necessary long apprenticeship,
that journey of perpetual discovery
and re-discovery, by which

the delicate, fragile, pilgrim self
pursues its becoming process
and graduates to be an artisan
of other castles in paint or ink or stone,
knowing they all begin and end in air.

Grave Swing

I found the unmarked mound
on which coarse grass and weeds were gathering;
the remains of two bouquets were rotting down;
some pale wild flowers attempted bravery—
it was my first visit after the funeral
to your resting place at Barton Glebe.
It seemed unreal to think of you below,
the kind of compost you'd chosen to become.
I remembered the casual chat we'd had,
we spoke of it like sci- fi or fantasy,
death seemed so far ahead, so unreal,
you wanted to be at one with earth you said,
not scorched by fearful flame; hence this choice
of woodland burial ground, even though
you'd never seen the place and never did.
Still, I'd hoped to feel your presence here
but it seemed a strange and stranger place.
Birdsong was punctuated by rifle shots
from the nearby army range;
ironic commentary on rest-in-peace.
Being alone I was allowed to weep.
I wandered away until I came
to the broad avenue of grass
where the groundsman-gardener-grave-digger
had parked his back-hoe and his truck.
He was practising golf shots down the avenue.
Seeing me, he looked a bit shamefaced
but carried on with a mighty drive.
It was then at last I felt you close to me.
Though you could never have foretold this scene
when contemplating bucolic burial,
I knew or thought I knew how much you'd laugh—
how the incongruity would delight you
the lack of reverence and solemnity

in a bloke working hard on the meaning
of life—the perfect swing and timing
to send a small white ball arcing through air,
straight and true between the groves of graves
towards no flag or final triumph at all,
a simple satisfying strike—just for the hell of it.

Flight of Fancy

When you were young before it all went wrong,
your dashing RAF cadet would call,
driving his racy Triumph Spitfire
to whisk you off to the Station ball.
On training flights, he'd buzz our house
salute with dipping wings and soar.

And then he died, your beloved man,
practising aerobatics in a cloudy May—
a high-speed low-level accident
all those years ago—and you were left
forever with what might have been
and sentimental views of uniforms.

My second time at your graveside,
it seemed too pat like some bad movie-scene
alone and wanting only to talk with you
when I heard the single-engined plane
over Barton Glebe. I saw the pilot
loop then flatten and flip a victory roll.

For a moment I thought the revenant
was reassuring me, not favouring you
with his display, as if to answer *yes*
to a query I wish I'd made but refrained,
worried it might seem too personal
or betray a mind knocked daft with sorrow.

As you were dying, I wanted to ask
if you found some comfort in the thought
of joining your first great love in some
fast beyond, the *lonely impulse of delight*
redeemed; the broken pact made whole:
imagination's lovely recompense.

Cavorting above the burial ground,
inscribing vapour trails across the blue,
the pilot left an airy scribble
fading like invisible ink—a child's trick
or adult conceit to make a secret sign:
the plane rolled again, then flew out of sight.

I'm left with absence and the mystery
of an imperfect metaphor for why I write:
the wish these airy trails of rhetoric
spun in a paroxysm of self-delight
could conjure you in an indelible salute;
the ink permanent, the magic absolute.

The Prescription

What is the difference between pain and discomfort?
the doctor asks with a sly smile probing my hypochondria.
A matter of degree, I reply, what I have is physical unease.
I experience indigestion plus difficulty breathing,
sometimes delusions: processing the idea my sister is dead.
(I don't mention my heart. Somehow it will mend.
From agony to ache—one day there will be scar tissue.)
The doctor doesn't say *Shit happens* but he might as well.
I've heard it before and see it in his eyes as if to say
it's only your sister. But I can't do shoulder-shrugging
about my childhood companion; supporter of my adult strife.
Our lovely friendship. And now she's dead.
I repeat stark words to make them real.
Still I can't believe. On random nights she comes to me,
sometimes in laughter, more often in tears, I wake to unreality—
blue spaces of sea and sky—the beach and purple mountains
shimmering in the heat. She would have loved it here.
I try to think her visitations by night are to comfort and console,
the harbinger of ghostly medicine; she wouldn't like me sad.
But then clouds roll in, the weather's strict changes blow through,
the storm hits, I'm blown off course, my unstable vessel tips. . .
The doc prescribes acid inhibitors thinks analgesics won't do.
Heartburn he can cure; the break must heal itself. As for pain,
nothing to be done but wait for more discomfort to set in.

Departure

How often have you read or heard it said
how lovely are the dying at their last breath
and afterwards how radiant their peacefulness?
Holding my sister's hand it was calm and quiet;
there was no struggle against the dark
just the merest lift of her mouth's corner
an expression of light irony I'd seen in life
with a modest shoulder shrug
as if to say, *is that it then, is that all,
I have to go? No choirs of angels
or blinding light only the merest sigh
and then goodbye?* I remember at the last
how strange it seemed you were still yourself
and there was nothing I could do
in that awful silence to change a thing.

The Sting

Six years on, I wake from a hymnal dream,
Death where is thy sting, where Grave thy victory,
to the image of you on that spring morning
approaching the ambivalence of Easter.
I was at the desk in your son's room
scribbling my daily words when you walked in.
I turned and saw you in the slanting light
still wearing your cotton night shift
pale gold against the dancing dust motes.
You smiled and said, *There are always nice
people in this room.* I knew you were thinking
of your grown boys as well as greeting me.
You sat on the bed with your knees drawn up
towards your chin; we exchanged more words
I don't know what about, but remember thinking
this is how we are—always easy together
and you looked so young it was impossible
to believe you were dying, even when the talk
turned serious and you said, *It's all crap really.*
I had nothing to offer to say it wasn't so—
I didn't speak for fear of sounding glib.
Now I wish I'd said how beautiful you looked
sitting there and how I would never forget
the sight of you and spend my life wishing for you
to walk down the stairs from your room
and interrupt me at my task. It's lonelier now,
though in all these pages I remember
and try to conjure you, pressing against
the knowledge loss is absolute;
you will never be here with me again
and there is no end to mourning.

Desperate Medicine

You had so many bitter pills to swallow
I bought you a box to keep them in,
on the lid the same *Tree of Life* design
as graced the tapestry you'd given me
some years before. It seemed an image
of affirmation, sentimental perhaps,
a reciprocal gesture between us
of the great *yes* despite your vicious illness,
its grim prognosis. Since you've gone,
I've looked more closely at that tree,
whose fruit is said to serve for food,
its leaves for healing, tried to see
how the forked and crooked branches
suggest our endless strife to twist and wrangle
the blight of suffering, so from new buds
might bloom the bright blossom of acceptance.

Olivia's Angel

For my grand-daughter

I place your present from *Nipperville*
to crown the plastic Christmas tree.
Appropriately, there is no proper noun
for the cardboard spindle of a toilet roll—
so easily it becomes a seraphic body;
from the hollow top, a bubble of woollen curls—
something out of nothing erupts—yellow, black and beige;
eyes are plastic beads below which beams
a felt-tip smiley face; a folded doily
fashions paper wings, the lacy pattern
making the idea of flight a holy miracle.
For finish, green paint and glitter-spray,
emerald, blue and gold, provide the illusion:
clothes and not clothes, heavenly raiment.

When you saw your creation there above
the lights and baubles, you frowned and said, 'That's mine.'
But no two-year-old tantrum followed,
as if you were content and unafraid
to leave your angel to decorate our season;
as if you understood the modest gift,
exercised or received, might illuminate
a love, a world, beyond possession.

Dream Mission

The shadowy line of people, hands by their sides
staring ahead, shuffle forward along a narrow gantry,
the roof low, stone or metal perhaps. It might be a prison,
the descent into a mine-shaft, or tunnel with no end.
The human figures are naked, gender indeterminate.
They have no choice. They disappear into the dark.
I am told to follow. Fear is a chisel riving me.
There is a sense of doom. No escape.
Yet I have a helmet lamp, which keeps slipping.
I struggle to adjust the beam. A voice from nowhere says,
'You must go on. You are the one with the light.'
It is then I wake strangely calm, thinking of the dead
who have preceded me in recent years.
I experience the rush of survival. Exultation.
For now, I am alive. Then I realise
the burden of the dream I'm not equipped to carry:
the responsibility to illuminate, to shine.

Last Letter to K

When I was young and at war with God,
faux Shelley with a roll-up and attitude to spare,
I had such anger with the crude theology
the local vicar preached, evangelising
his hopeless literal dogma of hellfire.
Desperate to believe but failing, I confessed
to the young curate, who suggested I might
volunteer to help the Third World poor,
donate my life instead of cash in a paroxysm
of compassion. At university instead I read
Non Serviam. In thrall to words' intoxication
bent towards not truth exactly but mind's
approximations, I sent you poems by post.
You said the envelopes resembled omelettes,
though you praised the flavour of the contents.
Theories I investigated. Marxian diagnosis
was apposite though his cure in practice
seemed worse than the disease. Still I became
an unsociable socialist thrown out of pubs
for singing the Red Flag, *Avanti Popolo*,
Irish rebel songs the night the Iron Lady
was elected. Downing pints of bitter,
I was radical, romantic, atheistical,
posturing, and often wrong, though Thatcher
was enough to dye the slightest pinko red.
I'm explaining, K, because you never showed
the slightest interest in politics,
I thought it was your blind-spot but maybe
you saw it was all about a lust for power;
love lay elsewhere. Losing you changed everything.
No politician's rhetoric,
no materialist philosophy had much
to say of help about untimely death,
sickness, loss and grief. Bereft I turned

back and found in flower's bloom
through broken stone strange metaphors
of renewal; saw there the need to re-build
another space for sacred—a means to praise
the processes of life, creative energy,
a new language of love transformed,
without possession, power-games, jealousy.
Impossible perhaps. Yet isn't that what we had?
Why losing you hurts so much? And isn't it
why benevolent orators lace their speeches
with, *Dear sisters and brothers,* as I wish now
I could address this to you and post it in one
of those clumsy envelopes and wait for your
sardonic reply? Perhaps it would begin:
Dear Brother, you haven't changed that much. . .

Aspiration

This is my ruined chapel
with words for broken stone
walls gesture at the sky
a fractured arch suggests
geometry perfected.

It is a reaching after faith
to transcend the mind's objection;
how the busy intellect can grind
all meaning to dust
no comfort in the choking particles.

So, I persist. I build.
Trowelling cement for the days
as if such work might hold
an echo of long-silent choirs
voices raised in faith and praise.

Climate Change

I moved into the sun from grey streets and rain.
Like a man starved of light I blinked, was dazed.
Now I am frightened of the weather.

The sky's uninterrupted height of blue;
the beach and hills resplendent in the blaze:
I moved into the sun from grey streets and rain.

And thought it freedom to stretch and bask
sans frost or wet in this warm country of the mind.
Now I am frightened of the weather.

The damp of England seemed a rotten history;
Australia's future light a shining promise.
I moved into the sun from grey streets and rain.

But now the sun's dictatorship begins,
drought cracks the earth, democracy wavers,
and I am frightened of the weather.

The heat strikes terror at the global hearth.
I moved into the sun from grey streets and rain.
Now I am frightened of the weather.

Dolphins

My first walk on the local beach
towards the breakwater, I saw them,
their mysterious loping arc through the waves,
sleek and elegant yet strangely substantial;

and I thought of you, how you would
love it here, walking with me, speaking
of how far we've come, and what strange
journeys we've been through to arrive

at this place where it seems
nature has arranged a greeting
that I might feel your mysterious presence
appearing, disappearing,

a playful salute which insists
on the kinship of all creatures
born into leaping life, plunging
between the light and the deep.

A New Start

We have come down from mountains of grief,
the cold peaks of morning, where light knifes the eyes
making rocky terrain sharp-edged, forbidding,
the vistas above and below fathomless and terrifying,
the horizon empty and severe.
We thought to reach the breathless summit,
dreamt of planting a triumphant flag of survival
with the proclamation, yes, *we have come through*.
Instead, we saw the fog come down, estranging and weird;
the only recourse to hunker down,
generate what warmth we could, tell stories of how
others have survived this fierce examination,
the clarity of loss; the loss of clarity,
blank vistas of no meaning, compass lost
and maps beyond reading.

We have travelled with no victory,
an inglorious stumble and winding drive
to the more temperate zones of the coastal plain
where we walk the beach and study the sea's detritus—
the seaweed necklace and the ring of shells,
the bleached bones of the downed gull
and the bizarre remains of jellyfish.
Our eyes search the horizon hoping for a sail
to speak of the onward journey,
and at night we sit on the deck listening
to parrots squawk and lorikeets chatter
while we drink our wine and watch the sun go down.
It's not that we have forgotten or ceased to mourn.
It is more we are letting ourselves be mended,
so when we wake bereft in the dark,
we hear the sea's insistent lullaby,
hush, hush and hush again it breathes,
soon you too will sleep again
and know your wandering is done.

The Limit

I wanted these poems to be about you,
an act of loving remembrance;
instead, in your absence,
their monologues play back to me,
looping to vacuity.
In our last times together,
so many silences I wish I'd broken,
though still I don't know what
I should have said of death,
trying to riddle hope from the
puzzle of mortality.
Now, I have words to spare,
I'm sick of the sound of my own voice
when all I long to hear is yours.

Afterword

Most of the poems in this collection were written in response to my sister's illness and death from pancreatic cancer in 2012-13. Karen was diagnosed just before Christmas 2012 and died in late June 2013. The grievous circumstances and multiple ironies of these events left me in a state of disbelief. It is perhaps not surprising, then, that the poems explore various dimensions of faith—secular, artistic and spiritual—in an attempt to wrest meaning from the blank of loss. The impossibility of celebrating or memorialising my sister successfully, much less recovering her through language, underpins the work.

In my experience of bereavement, I understood more clearly Joan Didion's account of grief in *The Year of Magical Thinking*. I found my previous interest in a materialist politics of social justice and compassion of little use or comfort in response to my sister's suffering and my own subsequent sense of disorientation. Instead, to my surprise, I found myself drawn to an investigation of various strands of contemporary theology. This was in part led by some of my sister's interests and by friends of hers who encouraged my investigations. In particular, I was drawn to the ideas underpinning process theology, an approach which also leads back to a progressive politics. I also enjoyed the writings of Karen Armstrong, John Selby Sponge and David Tacey amongst others. The ideas in this work were at a very far remove from the brutalities and banalities of the fundamentalist evangelism I rejected as a young man.

The act of faith required to write a poem remains for me a conflicted experience. Similarly, secure religious conviction eludes me. Doubt is ever present. The poems, then, are provisional statements. They are not written in support or illustration of any single position or belief. I hope they speak for themselves. Throughout, I have aimed for stylistic clarity and accessibility in the conviction that this does not preclude the articulation of complex ideas and emotions. I am not much enamoured of art that requires a theoretical treatise to make it intelligible or to excuse its opacity. I do not think this position is necessarily reactionary. If it is deemed old fashioned, I am happy to be so. I'm not interested in fashion. An inspiration for all my writing is provided by Brecht's lines: 'And I always thought: the very simplest words/ Must be enough.' I regret that many poems herein, despite my attempts, are not plain and simple enough.

Acknowledgements

I would like to thank the editors of the following publications in which a number of these poems first appeared: *Meanjin; The Best Australian Poems 2014; Dazzled* (Anthology of The University of Canberra's International Poetry Prize; 2014); *Grieve* (Hunter Writers Centre anthology, 2016); *Australian Book Review* (States of Poetry Series 1, 2016); *Axon:Creative Explorations*.

My title and the poem from which it is taken owe a debt to a phrase at the beginning of Marion Halligan's novel, *The Fog Garden,* where she writes, 'My grief is a great Cathedral...' I'm pleased to thank Marion for this borrowing, and for our long friendship over twenty years—so many wonderful conversations.

My grateful thanks also go to: Shane Strange for agreeing to publish this collection and for his initial cull of my unruly manuscript; to Penelope Layland for her incisive and challenging editorial interventions which have helped to improve both individual poems and the collection as a whole; to my niece Molly Caesar for the splendid cover image; and to Claire, who not only read and re-read the poems with a critical eye, but also lived them with me.

Notes

The Supplicants: Describes a visit to St Julian's Church in Norwich. *Hubble-bubble* was a sweet fizzy soft drink, which came in lurid colours.

Sweet Cords with Discords mixed be: My title is taken from the poem on the memorial plaque to Osbert Parsley in Norwich Cathedral.

O Tannenbaum/Wie treu sind deine Blätter: My title is taken from the well-known German carol and may be translated, 'O Christmas tree/ How loyal are your leaves (needles?)' Here and elsewhere I refer to Karen as 'K'—it was her chosen abbreviation with which she signed her letters and by which she was known to family and friends. Needless to say, it has nothing to do with Kafka and everything, in my mind, to do with *Special*!

Help and Self-Help: The Biblical quotations are versions of Isaiah Chap. 43 v.1 ff.:; David Gascoyne's *Christ of Revolution and of Poetry* appears in his poem *Ecce Homo* in *Collected Poems,* Oxford University Press, 1965 (1978), p.46

Archaeology of Belief, Anglesey: Two Variations: Llanddwyn Island is a small island off the larger island of Anglesey in North Wales. Llanddwyn in Welsh means Church of Dwynwen. St Dwynwen is the Welsh patron saint of lovers.

A Gift Returned: The italicised lines of poetry are taken from William Morris's, *Flora,* which appears on the tapestry referred to.

Flight of Fancy: *lonely impulse of delight* are words taken from W.B. Yeats, *An Irish Airman foresees his death,* a poem admired by Karen and her 'dashing RAF Cadet'.

A New Start: The phrase, *we have come through,* echoes the title of D.H. Lawrence's 1917 book of poems, *Look! We have Come Through!*

www.ingramcontent.com/pod-product-compliance
Lightning Source LLC
Chambersburg PA
CBHW020330010526
44107CB00054B/2060